dear
world

takayo noda

PUFFIN BOOKS

I would like to thank
Lauri Hornik, Nancy Leo-Kelly, and Atha Tehon
for their great professionalism and support on this project

PUFFIN BOOKS
Published by Penguin Group
Penguin Young Readers Group,
345 Hudson Street, New York, New York 10014, U.S.A.
Penguin Books Ltd, 80 Strand, London WC2R ORL, England
Penguin Books Australia Ltd, 250 Camberwell Road, Camberwell, Victoria 3124, Australia
Penguin Books Canada Ltd, 10 Alcorn Avenue, Toronto, Ontario, Canada M4V 3B2
Penguin Group (NZ), cnr Airborne and Rosedale Roads, Albany, Auckland 1310, New Zealand

First published in the United States of America by Dial Books for Young Readers,
a division of Penguin Putnam Inc., 2003
Published by Puffin Books, a division of Penguin Young Readers Group, 2005

3 5 7 9 10 8 6 4 2

THE LIBRARY OF CONGRESS HAS CATALOGED THE DIAL EDITION AS FOLLOWS:
Noda, Takayo.
Dear world / Takayo Noda
p. cm.
ISBN 0-8037-2644-9 (hc)
1. Nature—Juvenile poetry. 2. Children's poetry, American.
[1. Nature—Poetry. 2. American poetry.] I. Title.
PS3564.O285 D4 2003
811'.6—dc21   00-047500

Puffin Books ISBN 0-14-240280-X

The collage artwork for this book was prepared using watercolor paint
on handmade paper and Fabriano hot- and cold-press paper.

Manufactured in China
Text set in Adobe Garamond
Designed by Nancy R. Leo-Kelly

dear world

please tell me
why and how
you grow
delicious berries
and fruit in the trees

please tell me
why and how
you give
sweet smells
to the flowers

please tell me
why and how
you change
the colors of leaves
in the fall

please tell me
why and how
you keep our earth
so beautiful

please tell me

dear bird

I see you
sleeping alone
on the rooftop

your beak is red
feathers are blue
they are shining and
reflecting in the moonlight

once I heard an opera singer
singing
she was so colorful
so beautiful
she was trilling
on very high notes
as if she were
a bird in the forest

when the sun rises
in the morning
would you trill for me?

I will open the window
and wait for you to perform

good night
colorful beautiful bird

dear dawn

you woke me
without sound
streaming your twilight
through the window

the birds are
still asleep
the frogs and
the insects
have stopped
their choruses
as they wait for
the sun to rise

I too will keep
silent
till the morning
stirs with
the cheerful rhythm
of my mother's tiptoes

then I will hop
out of my bed
as my nose
tingles with
the delicious smell
of pancakes

dear apples

high on the ladder
I try to pick you
you are plump
in the tree
your leaves
tickle my face

when I have
that first bite
your tart and
sweet juice
journeys into
my belly
and tingles there

you make me
heavenly happy
my cheeks shine
as red as you

dear turtle

the many leaves fell
from the trees yesterday
and I was very sad
for I could not find you

when I thought of you
walking all alone
in a strange place
tears came
streaming down my face

I felt very blue
till I found you
in the leaves outside

my mother said
my tears made
everybody feel
very blue
(I am sorry, everybody)

please, my little turtle
please don't get lost again

dear car

you are sitting without wheels
at the end of a farmyard

only a few birds and insects
keep you company

I feel sorry that
you cannot drive out to see
the beautiful spring field

why don't you
have a dream tonight
a dream of having wings?

they will take you
high in the sky

you will fly
over the beautiful field
filled with buttercups and daisies

you will fly
over the whole wide world

you will not need wheels
if you have wings

I wish you wings
in your dream tonight

dear ocean

please leave the doors open
the houses are for small fish
living deep in your water

when a large fish
tries to catch them
they need shelter
to be safe and sound

when the water becomes
too cold in winter
they need shelter
to be warm and cozy

when they are tired
they need shelter
to take a nap and rest

please leave the doors open
the houses are for small fish
living deep in your water

dear snow

I see you
spinning and dancing
just like angels in white

I know
you want me to make
a tall fat snowman
with a long funny
carrot nose

I am sorry for
my cold
I cannot go out
I cannot make
a snowman today

instead
I will watch you
spinning and dancing
and I will think about
playing with you

will you please
come back tomorrow?

dear valentines

my grandmother said
"I love you
you are my valentine"
and she gave me
a box of
heart-shaped chocolate

before I went to bed
I ate them all by mistake

I dreamed
a heart-shaped moon
heart-shaped trees
heart-shaped flowers

and I heard them
saying to me
"we love you
you are our valentine"

dear fish

sky is
red
houses are
red
flowers are
red
you are
red
I am
red

everything is
red
in the sunset

it is magic

I wish you a magical swim

dear sun

I know
when you are happy
because you shine
and bounce
on everything

I know
when you are sad
because you become
hazy and fuzzy
as if you had
tears in your eyes

I know
when you are angry
because you hide behind
the dark cloud and
shout thunder
and lightning

I know
when you are happy again
because you stop hiding
and give us a wink
over the beautiful rainbow

dear trees

my father promised
to build
a tree house
for me
as soon as
spring arrived

I have drawn
five tree houses

but spring is
almost here and
I cannot decide
which one I like
the best

could you please
pick the one
you prefer?
it would be
a great help
to me

thank you in advance

dear tulips

you are
red
yellow
orange
just like my lollipops

please fill
my whole house
today
because my mother
is not feeling well

you will
make her better
for she loves
flowers

please tell me
that you'll come

dear stars

you are twinkling
in the moonlight
deep
deep in the dark
but clear sky

I lie in a hammock
between the trees

I can hear insects
and cool breezes
bring the smell
of mountain

I watch you twinkling
for the longest time
until
my mother calls me

in my bed
when I close my eyes
you still twinkle
inside them